Burton-on

on old picture po:

Mark Bown

Designed and Published by
Reflections of a Bygone Age,
Keyworth, Nottingham

1. Burton-on-Trent Co-operative Society branch no.4 was in Uxbridge Street. This view, taken early this century, shows the staff outside the butchery and grocery departments.

ISBN 0 946245 93 2

Printed by
Adlard Print and Typesetting Services,
Ruddington, Notts.

£3.50

INTRODUCTION

Burton-on-Trent is famous for its beer, the water being ideally suited for the brewing industry. The town boomed with the introduction of the Bond End canal in 1770. This was to join up with the Trent and Mersey canal in 1777, making Burton an inland port for a period. The opening of the Derby to Birmingham Railway in 1839 also opened up outlets for expansion. The town received a charter of incorporation in 1878, and was granted County Borough status in 1901.

The purpose of this book is to portray Burton-on-Trent through the medium of picture postcards, which were at the height of their popularity in Edwardian times – both as items on which to send messages and as pictures to collect.

Picture Postcards were first published in Britain in 1894, but it was not until a decade later that they began to take off, when in 1902 the Post Office allowed a message to be written on the address side. This meant that the whole of the one side was available for the picture, which obviously gave more scope to the publishers.

Photographic viewcards became very popular and the postcard became the most important way of communicating news or messages in much the same way as the telephone is used today. The years up to 1914 were the `Golden Age' of picture postcards, when millions of cards portraying every imaginable subject were published by a host of national and local firms. Hardly a village or hamlet was not documented at that time by a postcard publisher, though sometimes the number of cards available was unrelated to the size of a community.

The majority of cards illustrated were published by local firms, which was only to be expected. Prominent among these were J.S. Simnett, E. Abrahams, W.B. Darley, Tresises, Whitehurst, Siddals of Newhall and F.W. Scarratt of Derby. These photographers set out to record life as it was, and the postcards they produced have left us a marvellous record of fashion, leisure and work activities, shops and markets. Publishers are mentioned in the text where the origin of the card is known.

Many of the postcards featured have never before been seen in print, and I hope the book will give many people a chance to re-live a few memories of times and scenes that no longer exist, as well as showing younger people what Burton was like earlier this century.

Mark Bown
December 1994

If any readers have postcards, photographs for sale or loan, or other information which might be useful for future publications, please contact me at 30 Victoria Road, Ibstock (01530-262360).

Front cover: High Street, Burton-on-Trent. A steam traction engine passes Radford's bread van near the Market Place. Ellis's clothiers on the right was rebuilt in 1908. Card published c.1905 by Boots the chemist, and posted to Derby in December 1908.
Back cover (top): Eight Bass locomotives are featured on this card of the locomotive sheds just off Guild Street. W.H. Smith postcard, sent from Burton in October 1911.
    (bottom): the *Burton Daily Mail* of 29th September 1909 is portrayed in this 'still life' postcard which also shows a bottle of Bass, bread & cheese, and a beer barrel.

S 9195   BURTON-ON-TRENT STATION

2. The present Burton railway station was built in 1883, replacing the original site which lay just to the north. On this postcard, published by W.H. Smith in their 'Kingsway' series about 1910, a Midland train is picking up passengers on the Birmingham platform, while the freight train on the left is fully laden with beer barrels. Burton station was completely modernised in 1971.

J.S.SIMNETT   BURTON·ON·TRENT

3. The Burton Police Division tug-of-war team proudly pose on a 1920 postcard published by local photographer J.S. Simnett. Until 1910, the old police station stood on the corner of Station Street and Guild Street. Then a new station and magistrates court were built in Horninglow Street.

4. A c.1920 view of Guild Street after the old police station had been demolished shows the Museum and Art Gallery which opened in 1915. It contained local natural history and specimens of Anglo-Saxon remains found at Stapenhill and Wichnor, and local collections and objects from the Victoria and Albert Museum. Also pictured is the Opera House which closed in 1934 and was replaced by the "Ritz" cinema.

5. This chauffeur-driven motor car (ownership unknown!) was captured on camera by J.S. Simnett outside his premises on Guild Street about 1914.

6. The Ancient Order of Foresters held their 77th High Court at Burton Town Hall in 1911. Allsopp's horse-drawn dray makes its way down Union Street, complete with portable bottling plant in the parade and gala which marked the celebration. The houses in the background have been demolished for extra car parking for the main Burton shopping area. Card published by J.S. Simnett.

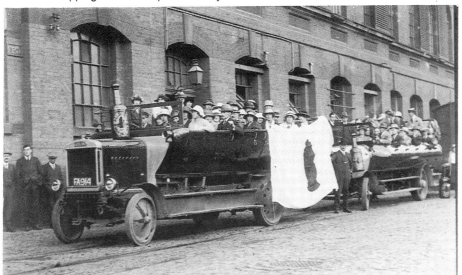

7. Trips for workers and their families were run by all the major breweries as an annual treat. This 1920s outing shows two motor charabancs about to leave on an Allsopp's trip. This company whose premises were off Station Street, amalgamated with Ind Coope in 1934.

Old Philadelphia Corner, Burton-on-Trent

8. Philadelphia Corner, as it was known, stood on the junction with Station Street and High Street. On the extreme left was Ordish and Hall, drapers. The shop covered in posters was once J.A. Longford, tailors, and the corner shop John Field, beer retailer. This c.1901 view shows the premises up for auction before demolition two years later after the tram lines had been laid.

STATION STREET, BURTON-ON-TRENT.   213112. J.V.

9. This 1930s view from High Street junction shows a bus picking up passengers in Station Street en route to Stapenhill. To the right is the "Wheatsheaf Hotel", Roberts & Birch (butchers), Fred Goddard's mantle warehouse, and the drapers Bradford Warehouse Co. Ltd. On the left is the Grand Clothing Hall, Hiltons, and Ordish & Hall. Card published by the Dundee firm of Valentine.

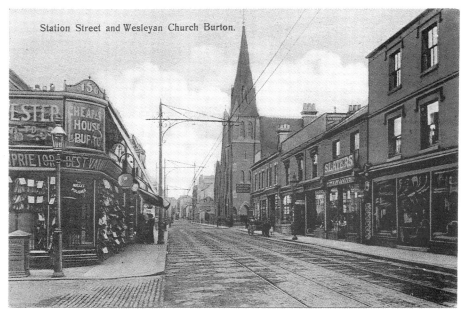

Station Street and Wesleyan Church Burton.

10. Wyles Brothers boot manufacturers stood on the left of Station Street, while on the right was Slater's grocery shop. Pearson Bros., drapers, was on the corner of Station Street and Union Street. The Wesleyan Church survived until the 1950s. An 'Ajax' series postcard, published about 1906.

11. A barrow boy waits for deliveries outside the premises of W.B. Darley – stationers, printers and bookbinders who also published postcards. To the right of this was Herratt (outfitters), W. Bellamy (outfitters), John Smith's laundry, the Post Office, and Whitehurst the printers. This view of High Street, Burton, was published by the Doncaster Rotophoto Co., and posted in August 1924.

12. The Grand Clothing Hall was constructed on the site mentioned in the caption to illus. 8. It was a fine structure, with total glass front, decorative ironwork roof and domed tower. The outfitters closed down in the 1940s, and unfortunately the building

has since been redeveloped. On this 1906 Simnett postcard, a corporation tram bound for Winshill is just about to turn into High Street.

BRIDGE STREET. BURTON-ON-TRENT. AJAX SERIES.

13. The premises of F. Keen, next to the Queen's Hotel on the corner of Bridge Street, have been demolished to widen the entrance to Wetmore Road. Another prominent landmark that has disappeared is the house on the approach to Trent Bridge: this belonged to T.N. Whitehead, town clerk. It was sacrificed when Trent Bridge was widened in the mid-1920s. Card published by Jackson & Co., Burton, in the 'Ajax' series, and posted to Eastwood, Notts, in 1925.

Burton-on-Trent. High Street.

14. A busy scene in High Street in 1903. Two drays are parked outside Robert Peck's pork butcher shop, whose premises were demolished to make way for the new Electric Theatre. On the left are Briggs (boot dealer), Mrs. Bounds' needlework shop, and Hallam the Chemists.

BURTON-ON-TRENT. HIGH STREET   66605

15. The Electric Theatre in High Street was opened in 1910 by the mayor of Burton, Thomas Jenkins, who was also the designer. It had a seating capacity of 750. The building jutting out on Station Street corner is the "Wheatsheaf Hotel" (formerly the inn of the same name). The card was published by Photochrom of London in the early 1920s.

16. Soldiers of the 6th North Staffordshire Regiment march past Dale Street crossing after mobilisation for the First World War in the autumn of 1914. The regimental headquarters was at the Drill Hall, Horninglow Street. Card by Abrahams of Burton.

17. This 1930s view of The Hay and Andressey Bridge is taken from the top of St. Modwen's Parish Church. Most of the trees have been cleared and the Bass malthouses on the left have made way for the public library, opened in 1976. Card published by Valentine of Dundee.

18. In 1905 the Post Office was moved from High Street to larger premises in New Street. On the corner of Union Street is the new Baptist Chapel, built in 1883 at a cost of £6,000 but unfortunately destroyed by fire in 1966. On the left is the "Green Man Inn". Boots the chemists published this card about 1905.

19. F.W.Scarratt published this 1930s view of New Street looking towards Moor Street. The Christ Church vicarage and parish room were badly damaged on 30th January 1916 during a zeppelin air raid, in which five people were killed and several injured. In the foreground is New Street railway crossing.

20. William Bass first brewed beer in Burton in 1777, living in Bass town house on the left of this picture. This busy scene c.1904 shows a tram approaching from town, and two horses and carts outside the Bass offices in High Street. Card published by fine art dealer S.I. Lever from a Simnett photo.

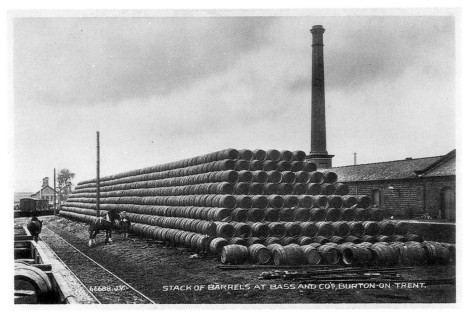

21. Casks at Shobnall sidings are awaiting cleaning and re-use by the Bass brewery. Pyramids like this became a common sight in Burton. Bass's other main stores were at Dixie's sidings on Hawkins Lane. A Valentine-published card c.1920.

22. A view of the Middle Yard at Bass, photographed from High Street. Beyond the bridge in the distance is Guild Street. The arched corrugated roofs are the cask washing sheds. To the left are the Firkin Sheds where nine-gallon barrels were cleaned. Note the overhead steam-cleaning pipes. The Middle Yard was cleared in 1966. Postcard published c.1905 by Simnett.

23. Bass's first steam cooperage was in Station Street, but was moved to the Middle Yard in 1863. It was powered firstly by steam, then electricity. The cooperage produced 1,000 casks a week until it was closed in 1966 when wooden barrels were phased out in favour of aluminium casks. Card published by Valentine and sent to Bognor in November 1909.

24. Up until the First World War the brewing industry had involved a male-dominated workforce, but as more men joined the forces women were employed to do all kinds of manual labour. The women shown on this Simnett postcard are working in the Bass Middle Brewery.

25. Train no.6 of a Bass trip has just pulled into Great Yarmouth station on 23rd July 1909. In total 9,000 employees and their families were carried on 15 trains. The annual trips were great social occasions, taking place from 1865-1914. Another Simnett card.

Burton-on-Trent. Breweries from the River.

26. Only the 120ft Bass water tower of 1866 is recognisable from the Hay now. The library stands on the site of the Bass Maltings to the left, while the old Bass brewery to the right of this c.1906 view has now been cleared to make way for the Meadowside Leisure Centre.

27. The Burton firm of George Orton, Sons, and Spooners Ltd., were famous for the manufacture of fairground equipment and amusements. C.J. Spooner operated from the Swan Works on Trent Bridge as a wood-carver, while Orton was a carriage-builder at 95 Princess Street. The two joined forces and set up business premises in Victoria Crescent. This Simnett view shows a newly-built showman's caravan being towed out of Edward Street into Shobhall Street, with St. Margaret's Church in the background.

28. Two new Sentinel steam lorries are pictured outside the works in Shrewsbury, ready for delivery to Marston, Thompson and Evershed's brewery in Shobnall Street, Burton. The lorries had a top speed of 12 m.p.h.

Worthington's Brewery, Burton-on-Tr

29. Worthington no.4 locomotive on shunting duties in
The photograph was taken just off Station Street lookin
site was cleared in 1968 and the Worthington Walk Sh

43526

ery yard. This Valentine postcard was published in 1905.
High Street. Worthington merged with Bass in 1927. This
entre is now here.

30. Another Sentinel steam lorry, this one made for the Burton timber-importing firm of J.B. Kind. In 1902, the company were at 156 Shobnall Street, later moving across the road to its present site.

31. The Burton Co-operative Society was founded in 1890, with main bakery premises in Byrkley Street. Shown here is the final moulding machine, which moulds the loaves before they are placed on movable racks and conveyed to the ovens. Postcard by J.S. Simnett c.1910.

32. A Burton Co-op Society van with two delivery men. The Society were the main local suppliers of bread and confectionery. Byrkley Street stores were demolished in 1975.

33. "Stop me and buy one". A Burton Co-op Dairy Department ice-cream seller stops to serve a customer in the 1930s.

34. In June 1908 the Women's Co-operative Guild held their 25th anniversary Congress at Burton Town Hall. These fashion-conscious lady delegates are in Rangemore Street at the rear of the Town Hall, and were photographed by J.S. Simnett.

35. A view from the top of St. Paul's Church shows the Town Hall as it looked around 1902. The properties at bottom right were cleared to create King Edward Place. Ind Coope brewery is top left, and to the right is the railway station. Card published by S.I. Lever and posted from Bangor back to Burton in June 1909.

J.S.SIMNETT Photo — UNVEILING of THE LORD BURTON STATUE — BURTON-on-TRENT.

36. The unveiling of the Lord Burton statue by the Earl of Dartmouth on 13th May 1911 was a big social occasion. Children are marching past the statue in King Edward Place. On the corners of Borough Road are Bailey's confectioners and Wilkinson's grocers. Another Simnett postcard.

37. In 1911 the borough's gas department illuminated the Town Hall with lights for the coronation of King George V and Queen Mary. Note the Midland Railway horse-drawn express parcels van outside the decorated town Hall. St. Paul's church is behind the newly-unveiled Lord Burton statue. 'Dorette' postcard series by Siddals of Newhall, posted to Peterborough in April 1912. *"This is the church I go to on Sundays"*, wrote the sender.

38. An interesting social history card by Simnett portraying voluntary cleaners outside the United Methodist Church at Winshill in 1912.

39. No.126 High Street, Burton, was J. Bassett's religious book, tract, and bible society depot. Just to the right was Brookes saddlers, established in 1795. These properties at the Bargates end of High Street have been demolished. Note the tram pole on the left. A Simnett postcard of c.1904.

J. S. SIMNETT, PHOTOGRAPHER   GUILD STREET, BURTON-ON-TRENT

40. The first Burton aviation meeting was held on the Bass Meadows from 26th September- 1st October 1910. The event was a great success and attracted crowds of 10-20,000 each day. Mamet's Bleriot monoplane is seen on this Simnett card, with Winshill Church in the background.

41. Only French aviators were used for the 1910 meeting. Seen on another Simnett postcard are H. Griffin, the official timekeeper. Madame Ladougne, E. Ladougne, M. Vernelen and M. Charley.

42. This photo taken from one of the planes in the 1910 display shows the industrial skyline of Burton. In the foreground is the corporation gas tower in Wetmore Road, while the spire is that of Holy Trinity Church.

BURTON OLD TOWN HALL.
Market Place.
Erected 1772
Pulled down 1883

43. This view from the Market Place looking towards High Street shows the old Town Hall, built in 1772. The pub on the left is the "Man in the Moon" and to the right is the "Elephant and Castle".

44. A large crowd gathers in the Market Place for the proclamation by the Mayor, Thomas Jenkins, of the accession of George V in 1910. This card was sent from Burton on 12th May 1910 with the message *"as promised I am on this somewhere but cannot find where."* Simnett was the publisher.

AEROFILMS SERIES   BURTON-ON-TRENT, SHOWING UNION STREET AND GUILD STREET, FROM THE AIR   No. 5819

45. Aerial view of the town by Aerofilms of Hendon in the 1920s. The roads down the middle are Orchard Street and Union Street, while the Post Office and New Baptist Chapel can be seen in New Street. Duke Street Midland branch railway led into Bass's new brewery (top left). The breweries were dependent on the internal railway system for their supplies of raw materials and delivery of beer. The town had a total of 32 crossings and over 87 miles of track and sidings. The railway crossings seen on this card are Park Street, New Street and Duke Street.

46. A view looking towards Derby shows the W.H. Smith bookstall on Burton station. A small boy browses through the postcards where this card (published by WHS) and many other local views could be bought. Also on the station were refreshment and

RTON-ON-TRENT.

dining rooms. This 'Kingsway' series card was posted from Lichfield to Melbourne in May 1917.

47. A busy Market day scene. The premises on the right made way for the Abbey Arcade block. Top right is the "Man in the Moon" pub, Brown the butchers, Draper's glass and china dealers, and Oliver's butchers. St. Modwen Parish Church in the background was built between 1719 and 1726. Card published by Boots in their 'Pelham' series.

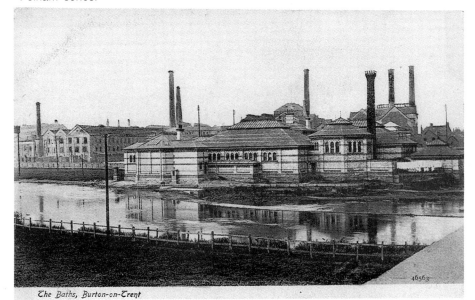

The Baths, Burton-on-Trent

48. The public swimming baths were on a piece of land called The Hay by the side of Trent Bridge. Built in 1872, they were donated by the Ratcliffe family. In 1980 the baths closed, to be replaced by a leisure centre.

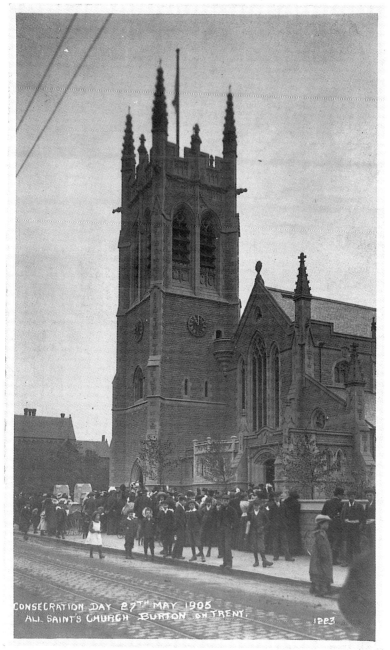

49. Local people join together at All Saints Church in Branston Road on Consecration Day, 27th May 1905. The church was erected between 1903-5 at a cost of £30,000, with money provided by Sir William A.H. Bass. The postcard was published by J.S. Simnett.

50. A rowing club has been in Burton since the middle of the 19th century. This view on a Rotary Photo Co. postcard, taken from Trent Bridge, shows the river and boathouses. It was posted to Birmingham in August 1920.

51. Before the Ferry Bridge was constructed, the Trent was only crossable at this point by the ferry boat, a service established in the 14th century. The ferryman pictured is Jimmy Dalton and in 1879 over 18,000 people crossed the river at a penny a time. A Simnett postcard produced from an earlier photograph, and posted to Dublin in June 1905.

Burton-on-Trent, Ferry Bridge.

52. The Ferry Bridge was opened on 3rd April 1889, with Lord Burton, Michael Arthur Bass, financing the construction. This view across the Trent shows St. Peter's Church at Stapenhill. Today's scene is changed with the New Bridge opened in 1985, also crossing the river. Card published by Boots in their 'Pelham' series.

W. B. DARLEY, BURTON-ON-TRENT.

THE OLD BRIDGE, BURTON-ON-TRENT.

53. Until 1864 the River Trent was crossed by a bridge of 34 arches, built in the 12th century. Then it was taken down and replaced at a cost of about £22,000 obtained under an act of Parliament by the Midland Railway. This early print, published about 1903 on a card by W.B. Darley, shows the old bridge from the Winshill side of the Trent.

TRENT BRIDGE, BURTON-ON-TRENT. (6)   213120.J.V.

54. The Trent Bridge was widened to its present width between 1924 and 1926. Though the tramlines are still evident on this Valentine postcard of the mid-1930s, the last Burton tram ran on 31st December 1929. Two of the motor buses which replaced the trams are in the centre of the picture, while in the distance are the public swimming baths and the spire of Holy Trinity Church, landmarks which have both now gone.

NEWTON ROAD, BURTON.

55. The horse and cart rules in this 1905 view of Newton Road, Burton by F.W. Scarratt of Derby. The houses on the corner of Bearwood Hill no longer remain. It was at this point that a Burton-Ashby tram crashed at the bottom of Bearwood Hill on 8th October 1919.

ASHBY ROAD, BURTON-ON-TRENT.

56. A lone cyclist freewheels down a deserted Ashby Road, Burton. Tramcars of the Burton-Ashby Light Railways were planned to run up Ashby Road until objections from local residents. The tramway was eventually re-routed up Bearwood Hill Road and Highbank Road. Card published by W.H. Smith and posted at Lichfield in December 1912.

ST. CHAD'S CHURCH, BURTON-ON-TRENT.

57. St. Chad's Church in Hunter Street was built in 1910 at a cost of about £48,000. It was a gift from Lord Burton who was also a benefactor of the Town Hall and Ferry Bridge. Published by W.H. Smith in their 'Kingsway' series about 1910.

58. Holy Trinity Church in Horninglow Street was erected between 1880 and 1882 at a cost of £30,000, on the same site as the original church which was destroyed by fire. This unusual multi-view postcard, published by Simnett, shows many different rooms and also the vicar, the Rev. H. Travie Boultbee.

59. In 1002 Wulfric, Earl of Mercia, founded Burton Abbey. On this Boots 'Pelham' series card of 1912, the only surviving building, the Farmery – renovated in the mid-19th century – can be seen. The roof contains timbers which date from the 13th century. St. Modwen's Church and the Abbey Arcade now stand on the original site.